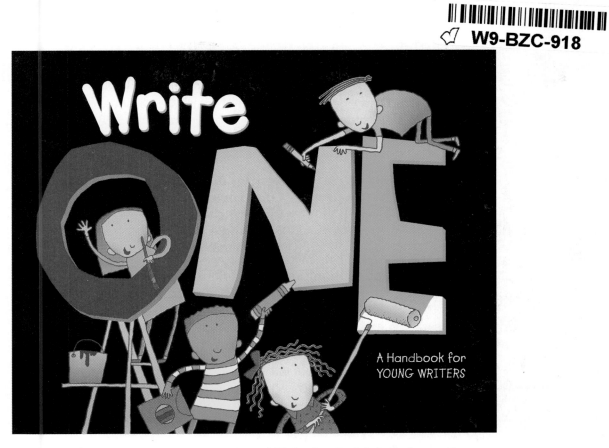

Write ONE

A Handbook for YOUNG WRITERS

Authors **Dave Kemper, Carol Elsholz, Patrick Sebranek**
Illustrator **Chris Krenzke**

WRITE SOURCE

GREAT SOURCE EDUCATION GROUP
a Houghton Mifflin Company
Wilmington, Massachusetts

W9-BZC-918

Acknowledgements

We're grateful to many people who helped bring *Write One* to life. First, we must thank all the students from across the country who contributed their writing models and ideas. Also, thanks to the writers, editors, and teachers who helped make this book a reality.

Betty Anderson
Jane Barbian
Betsey Bystol
Dana Callen
Sharon Frost

Nancy Koceja
Carol Luoma & team
Dian Lynch
Deb Pingle
Jacqueline Scholze

In addition, we want to thank our Write Source/Great Source team for all their help: Laura Bachman, Heather Bachman, Colleen Belmont, Liz DiBenedetto, Sandra Easton, Sherry Gordon, Bev Jessen, Lois Krenzke, Ellen Leitheusser, Shiere Melin, Tina Miller, Sue Paro, Allyson Shifley, Teresa Smet, Richard Spencer, and Sandy Wagner.

Trademarks and trade names are shown in this book strictly for illustrative purposes and are the property of their respective owners. The authors' references herein should not be regarded as affecting their validity.

Copyright © 1997 by Great Source Education Group, Inc. All rights reserved.

No part of this work may be reproduced or transmitted in any form or by any means, electronic or mechanical, including photocopying and recording, or by any information storage or retrieval system without the prior written permission of Great Source Education Group unless such copying is expressly permitted by federal copyright law. Address inquiries to Permissions, Great Source Education Group, Inc., 181 Ballardvale Street, Wilmington, MA 01887.

Printed in the United States of America

International Standard Book Number: 0-669-45975-5 (hardcover)

1 2 3 4 5 6 7 8 9 10 -RRDC- 02 01 00 99 98 97

International Standard Book Number: 0-669-45976-3 (softcover)

1 2 3 4 5 6 7 8 9 10 -RRDC- 02 01 00 99 98 97

Write One . . . You'll Have Fun!

The *Write One* handbook has four parts:

The Process of Writing This part tells you all about being a writer.

The Forms of Writing In this part you'll learn about writing notes, stories, poems, and more.

Reading and Word Study Here you'll learn the letter sounds and how to read and write new words.

The Student Almanac This part has pictures, names of animals and places, maps, math charts, and lots more.

3

Table of Contents

The Process of Writing

All About Writing

Rules for Writing

4

The **Forms** of Writing

Personal Writing

Subject Writing

Research Writing

Story and Poetry Writing

Reading and Word Study

Reading Skills

Word-Study Skills

6

The Student Almanac

Helpful Words, Maps, and Lists

The Process of Writing

All About Writing

Jenny and her friends discover that being writers is exciting. You can learn more and more about the writing process every time you write.

Jenny Writes

It's writing time in Room 101. Luke is planning a story. Rosa is writing a poem. And Ben is writing something silly.

Jenny wonders, "What can I write?"

Jenny asks Luke what he's writing.
Luke tells her he's writing a dog story.
It's about his three big dogs. Luke
knows a lot about dogs.

12

My Dogs

Jenny wonders again, "What can I write?"

13

Jenny asks Rosa about her poem.
Rosa reads it to Jenny. It's about the
time she went fishing with her grandpa.
Rosa's poem rhymes.

How we wish
we had a fish.

fish

Jenny still wonders, "What can I write?"

15

Then Ben pops up next to Jenny's desk.
Ben shows her the silly note he wrote. Jenny
and Ben laugh at the note.

Suddenly Jenny thinks, "This note gives me
an idea."

17

Just like her friends, Jenny begins to write and draw.

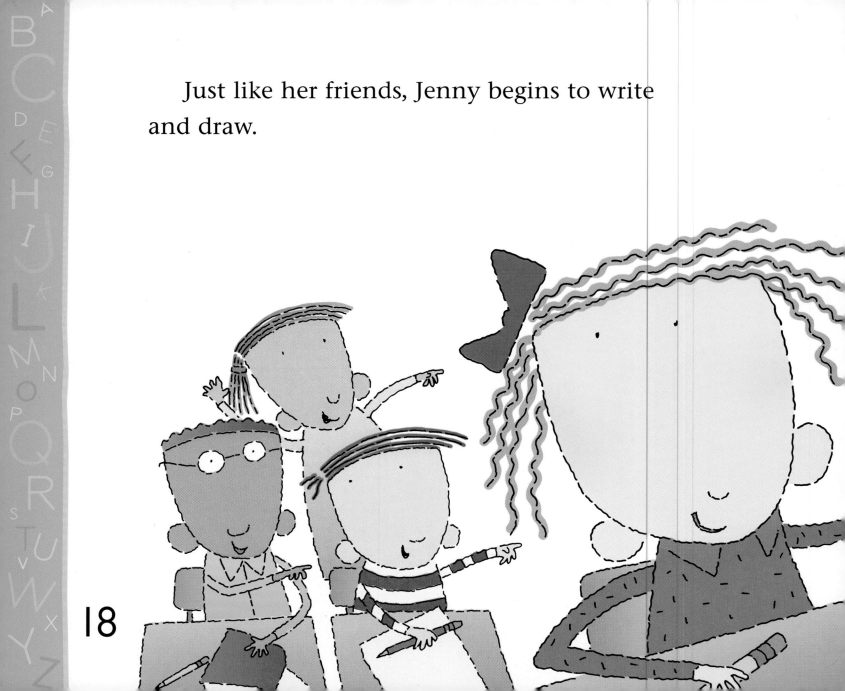

Jenny writes a note to her mom and dad.

Hi Mom and Dad,
I like cats.
Luke has three
BIG DOGS!
I wish we had
one little cat.

Love,
Jenny

Being a Writer

Being a writer means you do special things.

GATHER your materials—paper, pencils, and art materials.

WRITE about things you know about.

LEARN to use the writing process.

20

FIND ways to spell words.

- Say the words slowly and listen for sounds in the beginning, middle, and end.

/f/ /ĭ/ /sh/ → fĭsh

- Look for words in your classroom.

word walls   word books   posters

- Ask others for help.

SHARE your writing with others.

Hi Mom and Dad,
I like cats.
Luke has three
BIG DOGS!
I wish we had
one little cat.

Love,
Jenny

Steps in the Writing Process

The **writing process** has five steps: planning, writing, revising, checking, and publishing.

1

PLAN

- Talk.
- Draw.
- Think.
- Write lists.

Things Pets Need

1. food
2. water
3. love
4. a plas to sleep
5. toys

2

WRITE

- Write sentences about the topic.
- Spell words the best you can.
- Use your plan as you write.

Things Pets Need

Pets need food and water. Pets like to be loved. they need a plas to sleep. Pets like to have toys.

SPOT

23

3

REVISE

- Read it aloud.
- Does it sound right?
- Make changes.

4

CHECK

- Capitals
- Punctuation
- Spelling

24

Things Pets Need

Pets need food and ∧ fresh

water. Pets like to be

loved. they need a plas place

to sleep. Pets like to have

toys. ! fun

5

PUBLISH

- Make a neat copy.
- Share it with others.
- Put it in a class book.

Things Pets Need

Pets need food and fresh water. Pets like to be loved. They need a place to sleep. Pets like to have fun!

by Krista

25

26

Rules for Writing

All writers follow rules. When you follow rules, others can understand your writing. In this section, you will learn about rules for writing sentences, using capital letters, and much more.

Writing Sentences

A **sentence** states a complete thought.
You use sentences to write.

Mom made spaghetti.

- Begin with a capital letter.

- Leave a space between words.

- End with a punctuation mark.

Kinds of Sentences

Telling sentence

Sam ate the spaghetti.

Asking sentence

Who is Sam**?**

Feeling sentence

Sam is my cat**!**

Using Capital Letters

You use **capital letters** in your writing.

The **first word** in a sentence

> Bears catch fish.

Names

> Sandy   Trout Lake

The word **I**

> When can I go fishing?

Making Plurals

Use the **plural** form for a word that means "more than one."

Add **s** for most plurals.

friend — friends

Add **es** after words ending in *s, x, ch,* and *sh.*

glass — glasses   lunch — lunches
box — boxes   dish — dishes

Change the word for a few plurals.

child — children   mouse — mice

Using Punctuation

Use **punctuation marks** to make your writing easier to read.

Periods go after telling sentences.

Summer is the best season.

Question marks go after asking sentences.

When does summer begin?

Exclamation points go after sentences that show strong feeling.

Wow, it's hot!

32

Commas are for short stops. Commas keep words and numbers from running together.

Dear Gram,   June 13, 1999
I like red, blue, and green.

Apostrophes show left-out letters or ownership.

Gram can't wear Anna's hat.

Quotation marks go around a speaker's words.

Hannah said, "I like your new hat."
Anna answered, "Thank you."

33

Understanding Our Language

The words we use are called the **parts of speech**. Here are four of the parts of speech.

A **noun** names a person, place, or thing.

friend	park	apple
Dave	Grant Park	McIntosh

A **pronoun** takes the place of a noun.

I	you	he	she	it
me	we	they	them	us

34

A **verb** shows action or finishes a thought.

We picked lots of apples.
The tree was full of red apples.

An **adjective** tells about a noun or pronoun.

Dad picked the ripe apples.
I ate the biggest one.

The Forms of Writing

Personal Writing

Have you ever gone on a trip to visit someone? Have you ever been to a zoo? Just think of all the fun times you've had and the important things you've done. This section will show you different ways to write about them.

Writing in Journals

A **journal** is your very own place for writing. You can write in your journal every day.

- Write the date.

- Draw a picture if you want to.

- Write about things you do and think about.

38

Ideas for your journal:

- ▶ A story about a friend
- ▶ A wish list
- ▶ Something you like to do
- ▶ A place you like to go
- ▶ A poem
- ▶ Questions you want to ask
- ▶ A joke
- ▶ A list of books you've read

A journal is waiting
for your words.

A B C D E F G H I J K L M N O P Q R S T U V W X Y Z

Writing Lists

Lists are easy to write. They can be long or short, serious or silly. You can write lists for many reasons.

- Show what you know.

Wild Animals
lion
deer
snake
wolf
ape
hippo

- Have fun.

Happy Words
joy
sun
smile
jump

- Remember things.

Store

corn
milk
apples
peanut butter

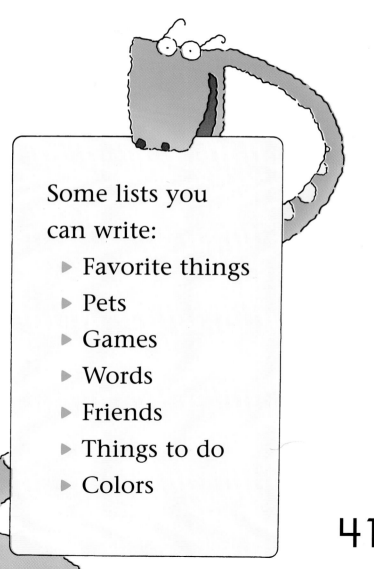

Some lists you
can write:
▶ Favorite things
▶ Pets
▶ Games
▶ Words
▶ Friends
▶ Things to do
▶ Colors

41

Writing Friendly Notes

Writing a **friendly note** is fun. Your note can be an invitation or a thank-you.

An Invitation

Lea,
You are funny.
Do you want to
play at my house?
Say YES.
Michelle

A Thank-You Note

Hi Michelle,
I had fun at your house. Thanks for the ladybug pin.

Lea

Other notes can say . . .

▶ Friendly things

▶ Kind things

▶ Funny things

Writing Friendly Letters

You can write a **friendly letter** to someone near or faraway.

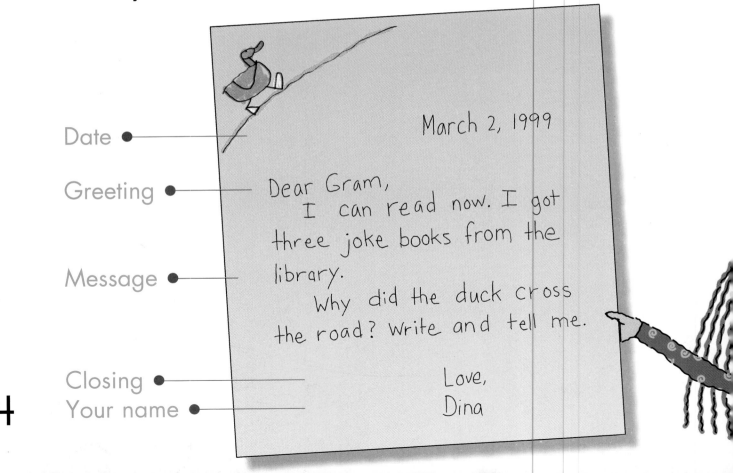

Date

Greeting

March 2, 1999

Dear Gram,
I can read now. I got three joke books from the library.
Why did the duck cross the road? Write and tell me.

Message

Closing

Your name

Love,
Dina

Sending Your Letter

Address the envelope. Then send your letter.

● Your address

DINA BENJAMIN
440 OAK ST
DENVER CO 80202

● Stamp

USA

MRS JUDITH MURPHY
86 PARK AVE
RICHMOND VA 23201

● Mailing
address

US
MAIL

Writing Stories About Me

A **story about me** is about a special time in your life. A cluster can help you plan your story.

A Cluster

Josh came home.

I held him.

a happy day

He didn't cry.

He was in a yellow blanket.

A Story

A Happy Day

One day baby Josh came home. He was in a yellow blanket. My mom let me hold him. He was blowing bubbles. He didn't cry.
by Jesse

48

Subject Writing

Writing about other subjects can be just as much fun as writing about yourself. You can write about different people, places, books, and much more. This section will show you how.

Writing About Others

Do you know someone you can write about?
Start with an important idea about this person.
Then write details telling about your idea.

Silly Nick

Important idea •————————— **My cousin Nick is silly. He puts**

potato chips in his soup. He wears two

Details •————————— **different socks. Sometimes he wears**

a bow tie. When he sleeps over at my

house, he brings his goldfish along.

Timothy

50

Write about . . .

▶ A special friend
▶ A favorite aunt
▶ A funny neighbor
▶ A famous person
▶ Your babysitter

51

Writing a Description

You can write **descriptions** about people, places, or things.

- Tell how something looks.

- Tell how something feels.

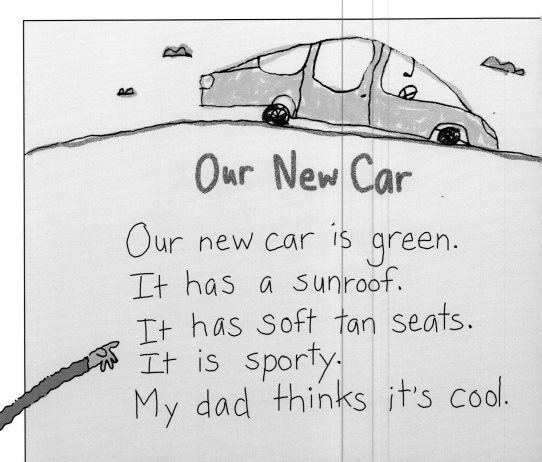

Our New Car

Our new car is green.
It has a sunroof.
It has soft tan seats.
It is sporty.
My dad thinks it's cool.

Use Your Senses

Pick words that tell how something or someone looks, feels, tastes, smells, or sounds.

My Grandma

My grandma
sings a lot.
She smells like
peppermint.

- Tell how someone sounds.

- Tell how someone smells.

53

Writing Directions

When you write **directions**, you tell the steps for doing something. Use *words* or *numbers* to put the steps in order.

Starting with Words

Making Chocolate Milk

First ● ── First, pour some milk in a glass.

Next ● ── Next, put 2 spoons of chocolate syrup in.

Then ● ── Then, stir it for 1 minute.

Last ● ── Last, drink it. Yum!

Michael

Starting with Numbers

1. •
2. •
3. •
4. •

Getting Ready for School

by Betsy

1. Wash up and get dressed.
2. Eat breakfast.
3. Brush your teeth.
4. Grab your schoolbag and go.

Other directions you can write:
▶ Taking care of a pet
▶ Making breakfast
▶ Making a friend

Writing Captions

Adding **captions** to pictures makes them more interesting.

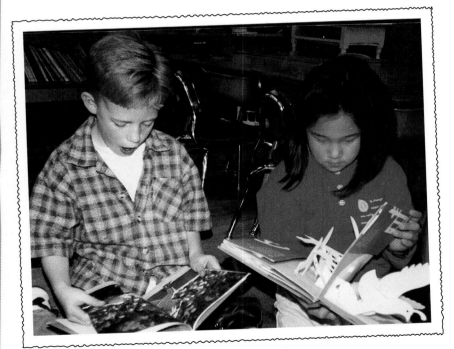

We love reading time.

Journals go everywhere!

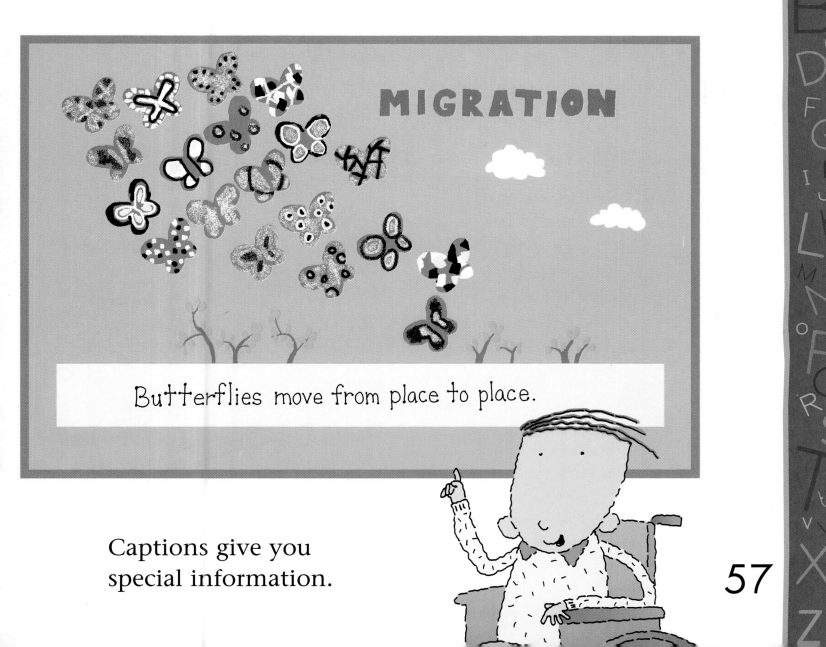

MIGRATION

Butterflies move from place to place.

Captions give you special information.

57

Writing About Books

Reading books is fun. Writing about books is fun, too. You can write a poem, make a poster, and do many other things.

Write a poem.

Book _Three Ducks Went Wandering_

by _Ron Roy_

One sunny day
the ducks ran away.
They wanted to play.

58

Make a poster.

READ
Sheep Out to Eat
by Nancy Shaw

It's very funny.
The sheep like green
food the best.

You can also tell about the books you read.

Do a retelling.
- Tell important parts and favorite parts.

Do a dramatic reading.
- Read favorite parts and funny parts.

60

Research Writing

It's fun to explore new things. Research means reading and learning about new and interesting things. It is exciting to write about these things, too. This section will show you how.

Writing Reports

When you learn a lot about a subject, you can write about it in a **report**.

1

PLAN

- Learn about your topic.
- List or cluster the important facts.

2

WRITE

- Use your list or cluster to help you write.
- Write sentences about the topic.
- Spell words the best you can.

Spiders have eight legs. Spiders have fangs. Some spiders are poisonous. Spiders spin webs. Some spiders live undrgrowd. Did you know that spiders aren't insects.

63

3

REVISE

- Read it aloud.
- Does it sound right?
- Make changes.

4

CHECK

- Capitals
- Punctuation
- Spelling

64

Spiders have eight legs.

Spiders have two fangs. Some spiders are poisonous.

Most Spiders spin webs. Some spiders live underground.

Did you know that spiders aren't insects?

5

PUBLISH

- Make a neat copy.
- Tell about it.
- Share it with others.

April 21

Spiders

 Spiders have eight legs. Spiders have two fangs. Some spiders are poisonous. Most spiders spin webs. Some spiders live underground. Did you know that spiders aren't insects?

by Todd

65

A B C D E F G H I J K L M N O P Q R S T U V W X Y Z

Making Alphabet Books

Making an **alphabet book** is as easy as ABC. You can make one by yourself or with your class.

- Choose a topic.

- List words about the topic for the letters of the alphabet.

Words About Our School

A	art	G	gym
B	bus	H	heart
C	calendar	I	ice cream
D	dancing	J	jokes
E	Eastview	K	kindness
F	friends	L	lunch

- Make a page for each letter.

- Put the pages together in a book.

E

G

F

We ha
on Tue
and it
gym f

H

H is for heart.
Your heart keeps you
alive. There are
good hearts in this
school.

Adam

ABC's
of
Eastview
School

A
B
C
D
E
F
G
H
I
J
K
L
M
N
O
P
Q
R
S
T
U
V
W
X
Y
Z

Writing in Learning Logs

You can write about your school work in a **learning log**. You can write facts, ask questions, and list new words.

A Science Learning Log

Day 1
Today we put seeds in dirt. We put water on top. We hope a plant will grow.

Day 2
The dirt looks black. It smells like outside.

Day 5
A little plant is popping out. Ms. Hill read us a plant book. Plants need sun, air, and water.

Day 8

The plant keeps growing. How big will it get?

Day 16

The plant is getting very big. It is 7 inches tall. It has many leaves.

Day 20

The plant is falling over. We need a stick to hold it up.

Learning logs help you remember things.

Ideas for your learning log:

▶ Backyard insects   ▶ Pet care

▶ Planting a garden   ▶ Weather

▶ Shadows   ▶ A season

70

Story and Poetry Writing

You have read or listened to many make-believe stories and poems. You may even know some of them by heart. Would you like to write some of your own? This section will help you get started.

Writing Stories

With a little planning, writing a made-up story is easy—and a lot of fun! Here are two ways to plan a story.

You can **plan** a story by answering questions.

- Who are my characters?
- What will happen to my characters?

You can **plan** a story by drawing a picture.

- Try telling the story in your picture before you write it.

Jake used a picture to plan his story. His story has a beginning, a middle, and an ending.

Beginning

Middle

Ending

Pumpkin the Cat

by Jake

One sunny day Pumpkin the cat sat on a rock. The rock moved! It was a turtle! Pumpkin got so scared, she ran away. She didn't come back until late at night. She never sat on a green rock again.

73

Writing Poems

Writing poems is like making little word pictures. Think of the best words to use in your poems.

Couplet

- Write **two** lines that rhyme.

> Sometimes comets in space
> Look like they're having a race.
> — Max

Triplet

- Write **three** lines that rhyme.

> Colors, colors everywhere,
> Colors here and colors there,
> Colors on the shirt I wear.
> — Shiere

Quatrain

- Write **four** lines.
  Make at least two lines rhyme.

Polka dots, polka dots
On my dress.
How many polka dots?
Can you guess?
— Kathleen

The owl in the tree was talking to me.
I heard him say, "Good night."
My sister says that owls don't talk.
But I know she's not right.
— Shavonn

More Poem Ideas

Tongue Twister

- Begin most of the words with the **same sound**.

> Jackson jumped
> and jammed
> just like Michael
> Jordan.

Cinquain

- Write **five** lines. Use the form below.

One word (the topic)
Two words
Three words
Four words
One word

> Shadow
> Tall, short,
> Hops, waves, jumps.
> Follows where I go.
> Me!

List Poem

- Make a **list**. Here are three list poems.

ABC's

Aunt
Bonnie
Can
Dance
Every
Friday

Ideas

Snow is everywhere.
  Snow is on our school.
  Snow is on the swings.
  Snow is on the trees.
  Snow is on the houses.
  Snow is under our feet.
  Snow is on our noses.
Snow is everywhere!

– Clarendon School
   Room 11

A name and describing words

Joker
On the bus
Silly
Eats cold pizza.

77

Writing with Patterns

You can write songs, poems, and stories that follow a pattern. Most patterns have rhyming words and a special beat.

Song with Pattern

The Itsy Bitsy Spider

The itsy bitsy spider
went up the waterspout.
Down came the rain
and washed the spider out.

Out came the sun
and dried up all the rain.
Then the itsy bitsy spider
Went up the spout again.

Rhyming words

New Song

Once you learn the pattern, write your own words.

The Friendly, Funny Lobster

The friendly, funny lobster
climbed out of the blue sea.
He crawled across the sand
and sat down next to me.

He reached out a claw
and then shook hands with me.
Then the friendly, funny lobster
crept back into the sea.

Here are some more patterns to follow.

▶ The Gingerbread Man   ▶ This Old Man
▶ Over in the Meadow   ▶ Miss Mary Mack

79

Reading and Word Study

Reading Skills

This section will help you grow as a reader. It gives you tips for thinking about your reading, for reading new words, and much more!

Reading to Understand

Reading takes lots of thinking. You should think before, during, and after reading.

Think Before Reading

LOOK over your reading.

- Check the title.
- Look at the pictures.

PREDICT what will be in the reading.

Think During Reading

TRY to picture what you are reading about.

CHECK to see if your predictions are right or wrong.

Think After Reading

TELL yourself or someone else what the reading was about.

ASK for help if you didn't understand part of the reading.

Reading New Words

There are many ways to read new words.

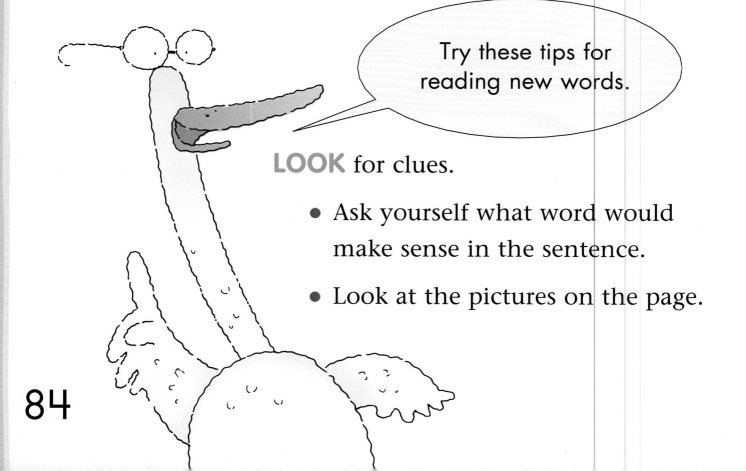

Try these tips for reading new words.

LOOK for clues.

- Ask yourself what word would make sense in the sentence.

- Look at the pictures on the page.

LOOK for parts or patterns you know.

- If you can read but, you can read butter and button.

- If you can read hill, you can read will.

- If you can read play, you can read playing.

LISTEN for sounds.

- Say the word slowly and listen for sounds at the beginning, middle, and end.

/f/ /ĭ/ /sh/ → fĭsh

ASK for help.

Using Everyday Words

Everyday words are words you read and write many times a day.

A
about
after
again
all
always
am
and
any
are
ask
away

B
baby
be
because
been
before
big
book
boy
brother
but
by

C
called
can
car
children
come
could

D did
down

E each
eat
every

F family	**H** had	**J** jump
father	happy	just
find	has	**K** keep
first	have	knew
for	he	know
found	help	**L** last
friend	her	left
from	here	let
funny	him	like
G get	his	little
girl	house	live
give	how	long
go	**I** if	look
going	into	love
good	is	

M made
make
man
many
me
more
mother
must
my

N name
need
new
next
night
not
now

O of
off
old
once
only
or
other
our
out
over

P part
people
place
play
please
put

Q question

R ride
right
room
run

S said
saw
say
school
she
sister
some
something
sometimes
soon
stop

T
take
talk
thank
that
the
their
them
then
there
they
thing
this
time
to
told
took

U
under
until
up
upon
us
use

V
very

W
walk
want
was
way
we
well
went
were
what
when
where
which
who
why
will
with
woman
won't
work
would
write

Y
yes
you
your

Z
zoo

89

Using the Right Word

Words that sound the same but have different meanings are called **homophones**.

ate, eight

> The rabbits ate the carrots.
> I saw eight rabbits in the garden.

for, four

> I made a card for Mom.
> Mom made four cupcakes.

hear, here

I hear Ben's cat.
The cat is here.

know, no

Do you know my name?
"No, I don't," said Theo.

read, red

Kim read a poetry book.
The book has a red cover.

road, rode

Emma lives on that road.
She rode her bike home.

son, sun

Mr. Kitt's son lives in Florida.
The sun shines a lot in Florida.

sum, some

The sum of 2 + 2 is 4.
Do you want some grapes?

tail, tale

A beaver has a flat tail.
Sometimes a story is called a tale.

to, two, too

Let's go to the movies.
I'll buy two tickets.
Can we have popcorn, too?

won, one

Brady won a gold medal.
He has a silver one already.

Word-Study Skills

We use letters and sounds in our language. Knowing more about them will help you read and learn new words.

Aa

alligator

bat
map
Sam

ape

cake
play
rain

Bb

butterfly

baby
balloon
bird
book
bow
boy
bug

Cc

cup

candle

cat

coat

cereal

cent

circle

city

98

Dd

duck

daddy
daisy
day
dinner
dinosaur
dog
door

99

E e

eggs

deck

Meg

pen

eagle

bean

Pete

see

100

Ff

fish

family
father
feet
finger
fire
food
fun

Gg

girl

gate

goat

gold

gem

gerbil

giant

giraffe

102

Hh

hat

hair
hand
head
home
horse
house
hug

103

I i

igloo

bib

hill

pig

ice skate

bike

pie

night

104

Jj

jacket

jar
jelly
jet
job
joy
juice
jungle

Kk

kite

kangaroo
key
kid
king
kiss
kitchen
kitten

Ll

ladybug

land
laugh
leaf
leg
letter
light
love

Mm

mouse

mammal

man

mask

milk

moon

morning

mother

MILK

Nn

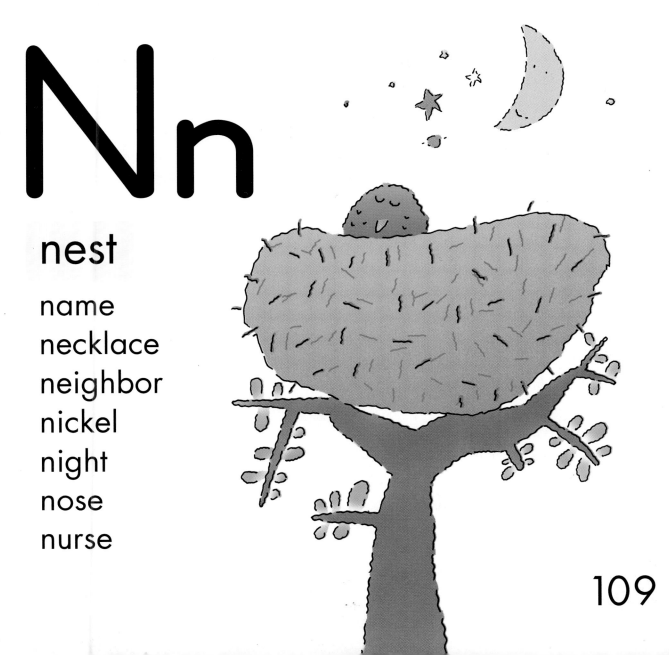

nest

name
necklace
neighbor
nickel
night
nose
nurse

Oo

octopus

box
dog
rock

oak tree

bone
goat
no

110

P p

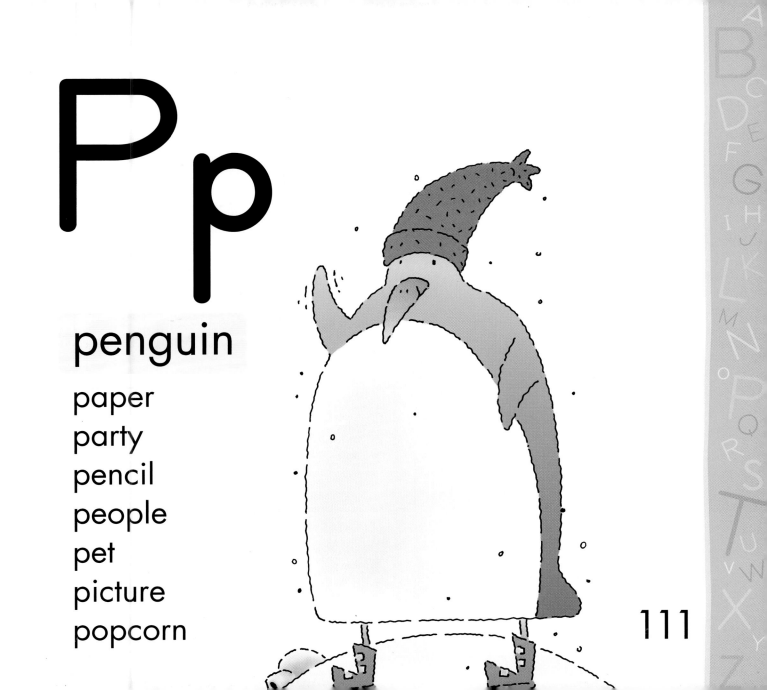

penguin

paper
party
pencil
people
pet
picture
popcorn

Qq

quilt

quart
quarter
queen
question
question mark
quiet
quiz

112

Rr

rocket

rabbit
rain
rat
ring
road
room
rose

S s

socks

sailboat

sand

seed

sister

soap

song

sun

114

T t

turtle

table
teacher
television
today
tooth
toy
turkey

Uu

umbrella

duck
fun
rug

unicycle

mule
Sue
suit

116

Vv

vase

valentine

vegetable

vest

vine

violin

visit

voice

117

Ww

wagon

water
wind
window
wing
wish
wood
worm

118

X x

bo<u>x</u>

ax
fix
fox
Max
ox
six
wax

119

Y y

yarn

yard

year

you

yo-yo

Sometimes y is a vowel.

Happy and **fly**

have the vowel y.

120

Zz

zipper

zebra

zero

zigzag

zone

zoo

zucchini

Consonant Blends

Consonant blends are two or more consonants that come together and keep their own sounds.

fr • pr • dr	friends	pretty	dress
bl • cl • fl	blue	cloud	flag
sp • st • sn	spot	step	snow

Blends at the end of words:

de<u>sk</u>   be<u>st</u>   pi<u>nk</u>

122

Consonant Digraphs

Consonant digraphs are two consonants that come together and make one sound.

ch	child	chop	chick
sh	ship	shop	shell
th	thank	this	thirty
wh	why	when	wheel

Digraphs at the end of words:

ca<u>tch</u>   ma<u>th</u>   wi<u>sh</u>

Short Vowels

Most words with short vowel sounds have this pattern:

consonant - vowel - consonant $\rightarrow$ **sŭn**

short ă	short ĕ	short ĭ	short ŏ	short ŭ
map	bell	pin	hop	bug
pan	pen	ship	Mom	gum

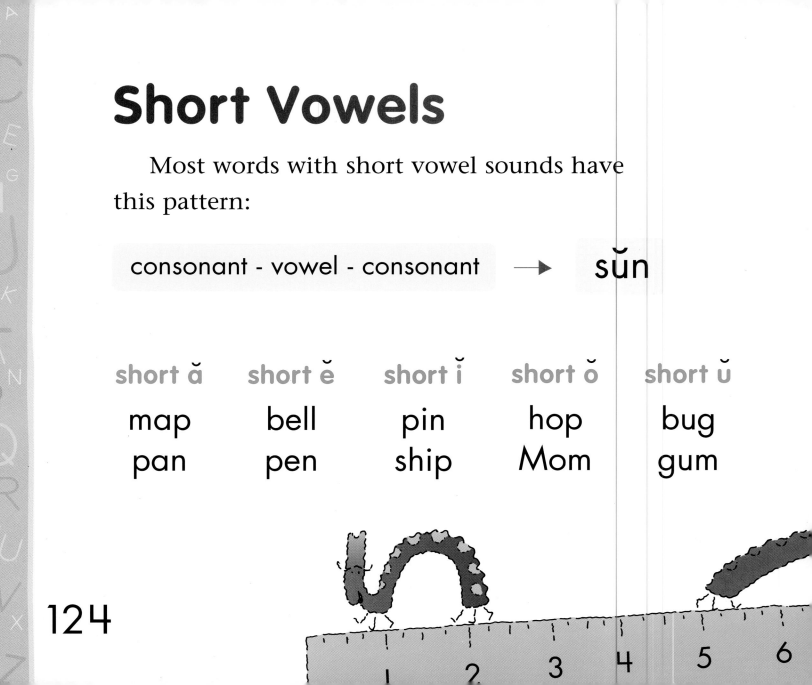

Long Vowels

Here are two patterns for long vowel sounds:

consonant - vowel - consonant + e → **cāke**

consonant - vowel - vowel - consonant → **sōap**

long ā	long ē	long ī	long ō	long ū
tape	Pete	bike	rope	mule
rain	leaf	pies	boat	suit

Rhyming Families

Rhyming helps you read and write new words.

If you know these words, **you can read and write these.**

hat	bat	sat	flat
fun	run	bun	sun
mop	top	hop	crop

If you know these words, you can read and write these.

fish	wish	dish	swish
cake	lake	bake	snake
like	bike	hike	Mike
rain	pain	train	grain

127

Contractions

A **contraction** is one shorter word made from two words. You leave some letters out.

Two Words	Contraction	Two Words	Contraction
are not	aren't	has not	hasn't
cannot	can't	I will	I'll
did not	didn't	it is	it's
do not	don't	you are	you're

Compound Words

A **compound word** is a longer word made from two shorter words.

Two Words		Compound Word
base + ball	=	baseball
fish + hook	=	fishhook
pop + corn	=	popcorn
snow + flake	=	snowflake
space + ship	=	spaceship

The Student Almanac

Helpful Words, Maps, and Lists

You'll love using these pages about theme words, maps, math, computers, and handwriting. This section covers all of these subjects.

Using Theme Words

This chapter includes word lists for important themes you will study in school.

Themes

▶ Calendar Words

▶ Numbers and Colors

▶ Seasons and Weather

▶ Places

▶ Plants

▶ Food Pyramid

▶ Animals

▶ Five Senses

Calendar Words

The name of each **month** and **day** begins with a capital letter.

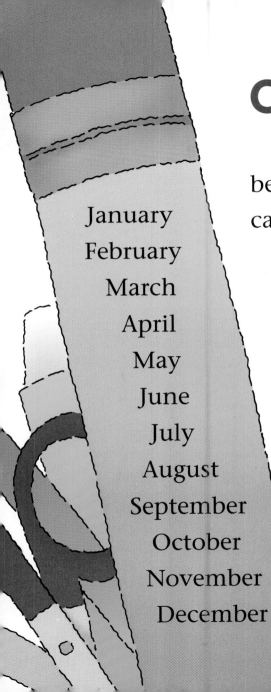

January
February
March
April
May
June
July
August
September
October
November
December

Sunday
Monday
Tuesday
Wednesday
Thursday
Friday
Saturday

133

Numbers and Colors

Numbers and colors are everywhere!

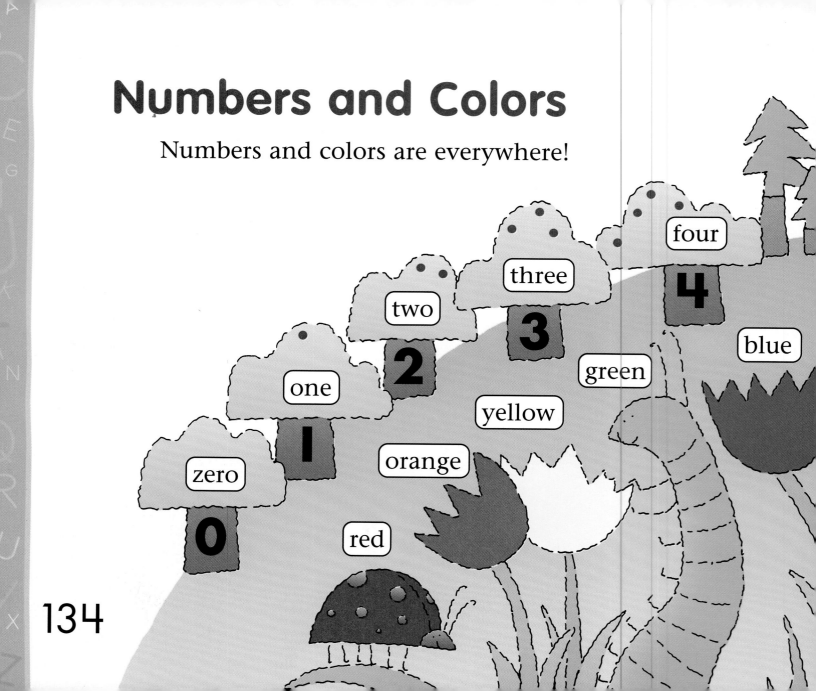

four

three

two

4

one

blue

3

green

yellow

zero

2

orange

1

red

0

five 5
six 6
seven 7
eight 8
nine 9
ten 10

purple
pink
white
gray
brown
black

135

Seasons and Weather

There are four seasons in a year. Each season has a different kind of weather. You use special words when you talk and write about the seasons and the weather.

Seasons

Spring

Summer

Autumn

Winter

Weather Words

partly sunny

sunny

hot

rainy

cloudy

snowy

cold

lightning

thunder

BOOM

windy

Places

Going places is fun!

mesa

canyon

beach

desert

mountains

hills

river

forest

valley

path

138

sky

island

farm

field

meadow

city

ocean

bridge

road

lake

street

highway

139

Plants

Many kinds of plants grow on earth. Garden flowers and leafy trees are two kinds of plants. These plants need sunlight, water, air, and soil to grow.

Roots take in water and food from the soil.

flower

leaves

stem

roots

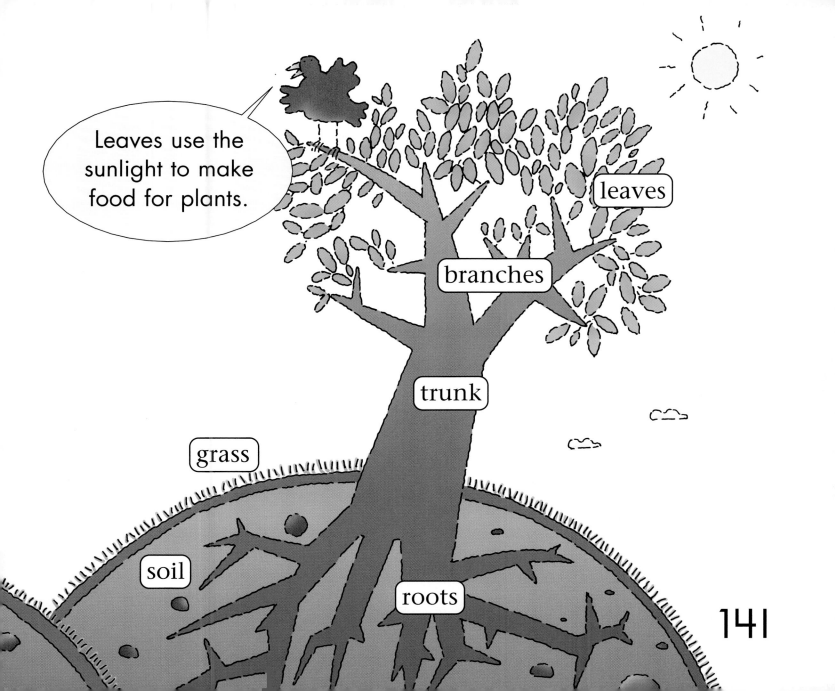

141

Food Pyramid

A food pyramid shows you how to eat right to be healthy.

Eat more foods from the bottom and fewer foods from the top.

meat, fish, beans, eggs, nuts •

fruits •

bread, cereal, rice, pasta •

fats, oils, sweets

milk, yogurt, cheese

vegetables

143

Animals of the . . .

Oceans	Woodlands	Grasslands
crab	bear	antelope
fish	beaver	elephant
octopus	chipmunk	giraffe
shark	deer	hippopotamus
starfish	porcupine	lion
stingray	raccoon	prairie dog
whale	skunk	zebra
	squirrel	

Deserts

bat
coyote
lizard
scorpion
snake
spider

Tropical Forests

ant
anteater
frog
monkey
parrot
sloth
tarantula

Polar Regions

hare
penguin
polar bear
reindeer
seal
walrus

145

Five Senses

I discover the world with my senses.

I **hear** with my ears,
I **taste** with my tongue,
I **see** with my eyes
    by the light of the sun.
I **touch** with my hands,
    along with my toes,
And whatever I **smell**
    tickles my nose.

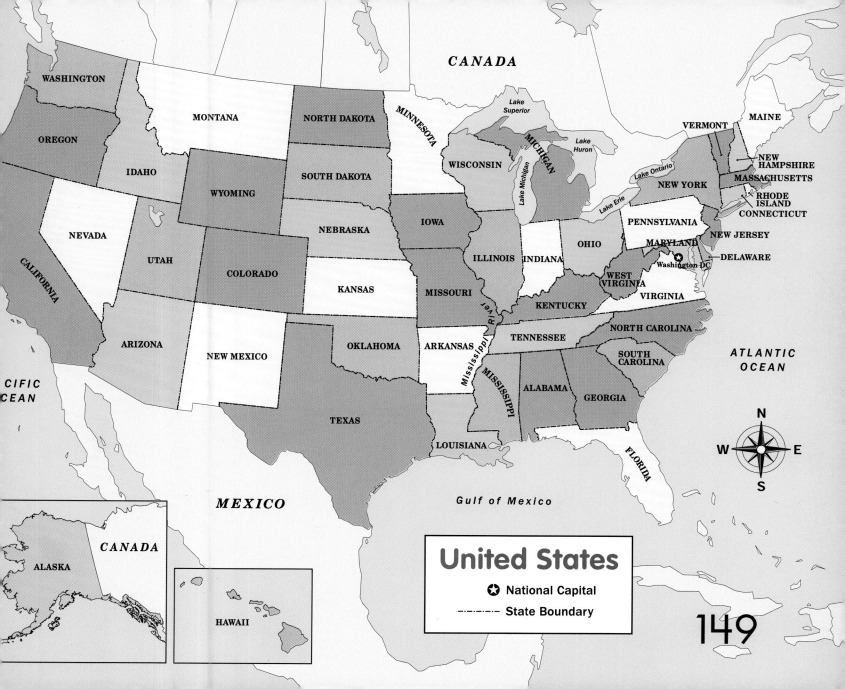

CANADA

WASHINGTON

OREGON

MONTANA

NORTH DAKOTA

MINNESOTA

Lake
Superior

WISCONSIN

MICHIGAN

Lake
Huron

VERMONT

MAINE

IDAHO

WYOMING

SOUTH DAKOTA

Lake Michigan

Lake Ontario

NEW
HAMPSHIRE

NEVADA

UTAH

COLORADO

NEBRASKA

IOWA

Lake Erie

NEW YORK

MASSACHUSETTS

RHODE
ISLAND

CONNECTICUT

PENNSYLVANIA

NEW JERSEY

CALIFORNIA

ILLINOIS

INDIANA

OHIO

MARYLAND

Washington DC

DELAWARE

ARIZONA

NEW MEXICO

KANSAS

MISSOURI

WEST
VIRGINIA

VIRGINIA

KENTUCKY

OKLAHOMA

ARKANSAS

TENNESSEE

NORTH CAROLINA

SOUTH
CAROLINA

ATLANTIC
OCEAN

TEXAS

MISSISSIPPI

MISSISSIPPI River

ALABAMA

GEORGIA

LOUISIANA

FLORIDA

CIFIC
CEAN

MEXICO

Gulf of Mexico

N

W   E

S

CANADA

ALASKA

HAWAII

United States

⭐ National Capital

—·—·— State Boundary

149

North America

ARCTIC OCEAN

ALASKA (U.S.)

GREENLAND

N
W   E
S

CANADA

PACIFIC OCEAN

UNITED STATES

ATLANTIC OCEAN

MEXICO

Gulf of Mexico

WEST INDIES

CENTRAL AMERICA

SOUTH AMERICA

The World
Continents and Oceans

ARCTIC OCEAN

ARCTIC OCEAN

NORTH AMERICA

SOUTH AMERICA

ATLANTIC OCEAN

PACIFIC OCEAN

EUROPE

ASIA

AFRICA

PACIFIC OCEAN

INDIAN OCEAN

AUSTRALIA

ANTARCTICA

EQUATOR

N
W   E
S

151

Working with Math

You work with math every day. You tell time. You count your lunch money. You add and subtract when you share things with your friends.

In this section you will find charts and tables to show you how math can work for you.

Telling Time

Face clocks show time with hands pointing to numbers. **Digital clocks** show time with numbers. Both of these clocks show 2:30.

hour hand

minute hand

hour • • minutes

This number changes every minute.

- The numbers on a face clock stand for both hours and minutes.

153

Numbers 1 to 100

The chart below will help you count by 1's, 5's, and 10's.

Hundred Chart

1	2	3	4	5	6	7	8	9	10
11	12	13	14	15	16	17	18	19	20
21	22	23	24	25	26	27	28	29	30
31	32	33	34	35	36	37	38	39	40
41	42	43	44	45	46	47	48	49	50
51	52	53	54	55	56	57	58	59	60
61	62	63	64	65	66	67	68	69	70
71	72	73	74	75	76	77	78	79	80
81	82	83	84	85	86	87	88	89	90
91	92	93	94	95	96	97	98	99	100

Place Value

This chart shows what each part of a number is worth.

hundreds	tens	ones		
		7	=	7
	1	0	=	10
	3	2	=	32
	5	5	=	55
1	0	0	=	100

7 = 0 hundreds	0 tens	7 ones	
10 = 0 hundreds	1 tens	0 ones	
32 = 0 hundreds	3 tens	2 ones	
55 = 0 hundreds	5 tens	5 ones	
100 = 1 hundreds	0 tens	0 ones	

Bar Graphs

A **bar graph** helps you show how many.

Children's Favorite Season

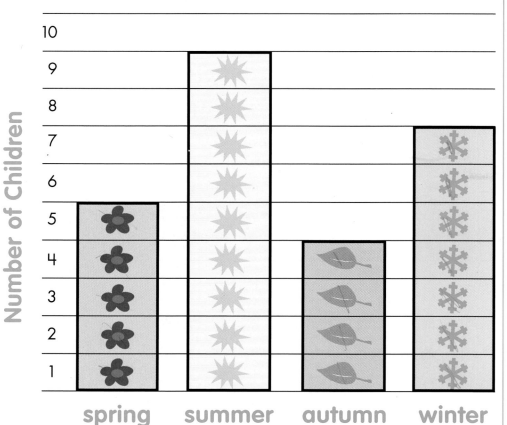

spring = 5
summer = 9
autumn = 4
winter = 7

156

Money

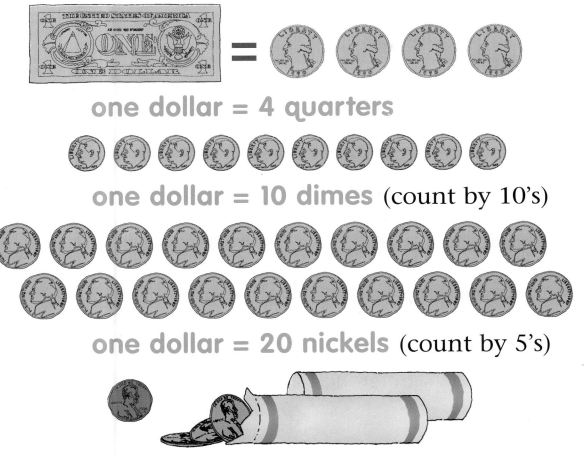

one dollar = 4 quarters

one dollar = 10 dimes (count by 10's)

one dollar = 20 nickels (count by 5's)

one dollar = 100 pennies (count by 1's)

Addition and Subtraction

Addition means putting numbers together.

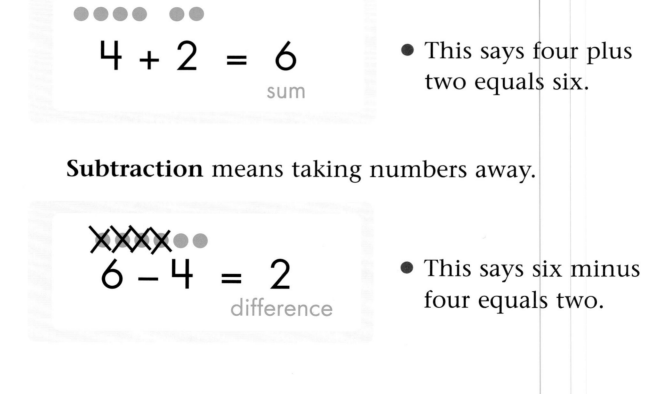

4 + 2 = 6

sum

- This says four plus two equals six.

Subtraction means taking numbers away.

6 – 4 = 2

difference

- This says six minus four equals two.

Fractions

A **fraction** is a part of something whole.

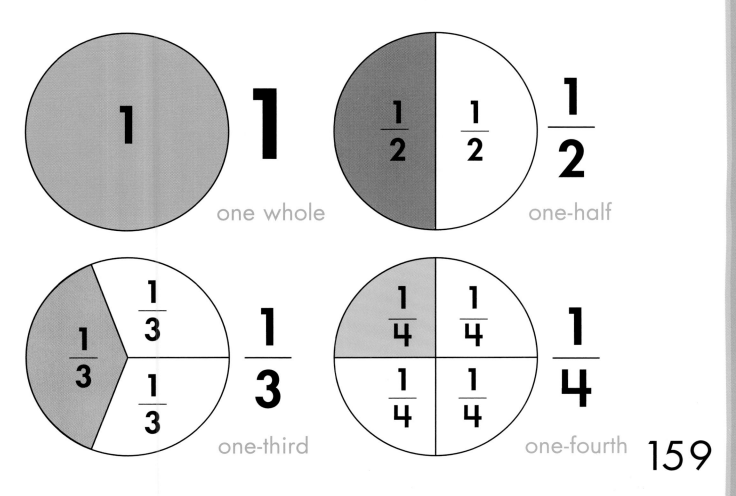

1 — one whole

$\frac{1}{2}$ — one-half

$\frac{1}{3}$ — one-third

$\frac{1}{4}$ — one-fourth

Knowing About a Computer

The more you know about a computer, the more you can do with it. You can use a computer for writing and many other things.

Parts of a Personal Computer

printer

mouse

Silly Nick

My cousin Nick is silly. He puts potato chips in his soup. He wears two different socks. Sometimes he wears a bow tie. When he sleeps over at my house, he brings his goldfish along.

Timothy

Silly Nick

My cousin Nick is silly. He puts potato chips in his soup. He wears two different socks. Sometimes he wears a bow tie. When he sleeps over at my house, he brings his goldfish along.

Timothy

monitor

computer "brain"

disk

keyboard

161

Practicing Handwriting

Neat handwriting helps you and others read and enjoy your writing.

Handwriting Hints

- Look at handwriting models.
- Practice letters often.
- Leave spaces between words.
- Slant all letters the same way.

Manuscript Models

A B C D E F G
H I J K L M N O
P Q R S T U V
W X Y Z

a b c d e f g h i j
k l m n o p q r s
t u v w x y z

163

Continuous Stroke Models

A B C D E F G
H I J K L M N O
P Q R S T U V
W X Y Z

a b c d e f g h i j
k l m n o p q r s
t u v w x y z

Index

The **index** can help you find information in your handbook. Let's say you want to write a letter. You can look in your index under "letters" for help.

167